The Rockwool Foundation Research Unit

Study Paper No. 72

Leading Public Service Organizations

How to obtain employees with high self-efficacy

Christian Bøtcher Jacobsen and
Lotte Bøgh Andersen

University Press of Southern Denmark

Odense 2014

Leading Public Service Organizations:

How to obtain employees with high self-efficacy

Study Paper No. 72

Published by:
© The Rockwool Foundation Research Unit

Address:
The Rockwool Foundation Research Unit
Soelvgade 10, 2.tv.
DK-1307 Copenhagen K

Telephone   +45 33 34 48 00
E-mail   forskningsenheden@rff.dk
web site: www.en.rff.dk

ISBN 978-87-93119-19-2
ISSN 0908-3979

August 2014

Leading Public Service Organizations: How to obtain employees with high self-efficacy

Christian Bøtcher Jacobsen & Lotte Bøgh Andersen, Aarhus University (contact: christianj@ps.au.dk)

Abstract

Public management literature has often debated the usefulness of transactional leadership. Some scholars are concerned that transactional leadership strategies will harm public employees' perceived competence (i.e. their self-efficacy), but in fact there are also arguments for the opposite result - that feelings of competence are strengthened by conditional rewards, because they provide feedback about performance. We study how 91 high school principals' reported use of rewards and sanctions affect perceived professional competence among their 1,921 teachers. The results show that the use of rewards strengthens self-efficacy, and that the use of sanctions does not seem to have negative effects. Furthermore, the teachers' self-efficacy can be linked positively to organizational performance. This suggests that rewards can be an important tool for managers in the public sector.

Transactional leaders use rewards and/or sanctions linked to effort and results to try to obtain better performance, and whether this leadership strategy is applicable to public organizations is a controversial issue. The assumption behind transformational leadership is that employees only exert effort if they are induced to do so by positive or negative incentives (Bass & Riggio, 2006; Holmström, 1979; Moe, 1984). In a public administration context, this assumption has been questioned (Kellough & Lu, 1993; Heinrich, 2009), because public employees can be motivated by many other factors than extrinsic rewards or sanctions (Perry et al. 2009). Some even argue that transactional strategies are harmful in public organizations (Moynihan, 2010), and a typical argument against the use of economic rewards in the public sector is the existence of autonomous motivation, which can be crowded out, if pecuniary incentives restrict self-determination and feelings of competence among employees. However, we only have limited empirical knowledge about how transactional leadership affects public employees and their willingness to devote effort through their work. Existing studies indicate that the effect might be neutral or even positive if employees see the transactional strategies as supportive (Jacobsen & Andersen forthcoming; Andersen & Pallesen 2008), and this could be due to the employees' feeling of competence and the effect of leadership on this feeling. A key question is, in other words, whether it is possible to use transactional leadership to obtain employees with high self-efficacy.

Although the field of administrative leadership has made enormous progress in the last decade (Van Wart 2013), we still know too little about important mediators between leadership and performance such as self-efficacy. Employee self-efficacy can be defined as the 'belief in one's capabilities to organize and execute the courses of action required to produce given attainments' (Bandura 1997: 3), and it has repeatedly been found to be closely related to performance at both the individual and organizational level (Bandura, 1997; Wright & Grant, 2010). Self-efficacy has been found to mediate the relationships between transformational leadership and performance (e.g. Pillai & Williams 2004), but we do not know whether the mechanisms are the same for transactional leadership.

The multiple performance goals in many public organizations combined with high levels of public service motivation (Perry & Wise 1990) have been argued to make rewards inherently difficult and potentially hazardous to use (Langbein, 2010), but existing studies tend to find that transactional leadership can have positive effects also in the public sector (Hooijberg & Choi, 2001; Judge & Piccolo, 2004; Lowe, Kroeck, & Sivasubramaniam, 1996; Oberfield 2014; Andersen & Pallesen 2008; Trottier et al. 2008). The reasons behind these effects might be increased attention to organizational goals and the fact that many employees have mixed motivation, combining a wish to do good for society and others with a wish to do good for themselves

(Le Grand 2003). If transactional leadership can have positive effects without impairing employees' perceived competence, it is very important to obtain knowledge about the mechanisms. Thus, this paper investigates the following research question: *How are transactional leadership strategies related to employee self-efficacy in public organizations, and how is self-efficacy related to organizational performance?*

Empirically, we use data from 91 upper secondary schools in Denmark. This encompasses survey data from two questionnaires to 91 principals and their 1,921 teachers combined with highly reliable register data regarding school characteristics and performance. Multi-level analyses show that the principals' reported use of contingent rewards is positively related to teacher self-efficacy, and that self-efficacy seems to matter for school added value to student grades. The findings imply that contrary to standard arguments in public administration, transactional leadership can be a useful tool for managers. Thus, the paper contributes to the growing literature on leadership in public management by exploring the often neglected topic of transactional leadership and linking it with both self-efficacy and performance. After the presentation of the theoretical framework and our three main hypotheses in the next section, we describe data and methods and present the results. Finally, we discuss the results, conclude and propose further research.

Theoretical framework

We focus on the use of transactional leadership, which in the business administration literature is seen as leaders providing social exchanges in return for performance (Bass & Riggio, 2006). Transactional leadership differs from transformational leadership, which is a contingency-free leadership strategy, where the leader seeks to stimulate and inspire followers to change their motivation and values so they increase their performance (Bass & Riggio, 2006: 3). The dominant theory on transformational and transactional leadership has been the Full Range Leadership Theory. One of the reasons for its dominance is its measurement tool called the Multifactor Leadership Questionnaire (MLQ) (Bass, 1985; Bass & Riggio, 2006). In this tradition, transactional leadership is seen as consisting of three dimensions. Contingent reward is the assignment or obtainment of employee agreement on goals with rewards for satisfactory results. Active management-by-exception is monitoring of deviances from standards, mistakes and errors, and passive management-by-exception is when the leader only intervenes when there are clearly visible deviances from standards, mistakes and errors (Bass & Riggio, 2006: 6-8). Many studies do, however, not distinguish between active and passive management-by-exception. The Full Range Leadership theory sees transformational leadership as consisting of four dimensions: Idealized influence, inspirational motivation, intellectual stimulation, and individual consideration. Proponents of the Full Range Leadership Theory expect that effective leaders apply both transactional and transformational leadership behaviors.

Over the years, the Full Range Leadership theory has received substantial critique related to its concepts, mechanisms and measurement of leadership (Yukl, 1999; Antonakis & House, 2013; Van Knippenberg & Sitkin, 2013). The critique has mainly been directed at transformational leadership, but some scholars have raised their concerns about the general framework. First, the definition of leadership has received critique for being elusive or even missing. The term 'Full Range' implies that it encompasses all leadership behaviors, but this is hardly the case. Second, the dimensions have received critique for being inductively constructed, but with little theoretical meaning and unclear relations. This leads to the third critique that even empirically the dimensions are highly correlated and often cannot be separated. Finally, behavior and behavioral consequences are inadequately separated, and it is especially problematic to have conceptualization confound leadership with its effects when we (as in this paper) study leadership behavior, employee outcomes and organizational behavior. On the positive side, a number of recent studies have demonstrated the relevance of these two leadership strategies in public organizations (Bellé, 2013; Moynihan et al. 2012; Oberfield, 2014; Park & Rainey 2008; Trottier et al. 2008).

Consequently, we use concepts transactional and transformational leadership in this paper, but we have developed definitions which separate leadership from its consequences and try to focus on the basic distinctions between different types of leadership behavior. We see transactional leadership as *the use of contingent rewards and sanctions intended to create employee self-interest in achieving organization goals*. Thus, we still stress that there are two sides to the transactional strategy – the whip (punishment) and the carrot (rewards). Instead of defining transactional leadership by its causes, we include intentions as part of the definition. We argue that the mere presence of systems of rewards and punishments is not enough: Transactional leadership must be intentional, meaning that the leader must believe that these systems motivate employees to achieve performance goals (due to self-interest), and use them for this reason. Intentions might be difficult to measure, but it is important to capture whether a leader tries to motivate and direct his employees through appealing to their own self-interest. In contrast, transformational leadership can be seen as *behaviors seeking to develop, share, and sustain a vision intended to encourage that employees transcend their own self-interest and achieve organization goals*. Here, the intent is totally different, namely to encourage them go beyond their self-interest and make them share organizational goals and thus try to obtain these goals because they are seen as desirable in themselves.

Our definition of transformational leadership is akin to, but still different from recent definitions of visionary leadership. Knippenberg and Stam (2014: 243) for example define visionary leadership as the verbal communication of an image of a future for a collective with the intention to persuade others to contribute to the realization of that future. It is similar to our definitions in its use of intention, but it differs in focusing only on communication (sharing) of the vision, while transformational leadership in our understanding also includes developing and sustaining the vision. Our definition also explicitly states that the intent behind the use of transformational leadership is to make employees transcend their self-interest. Our conceptualization is in line with other public administration studies, still calling the leadership strategy transformational and arguing that particularly the visionary aspect is important in the public sector (Bellé, 2013; Moynihan et al., 2012). Again, a transformational leader might not be successful in this (otherwise we would define behavior by it consequences), but similar to the literature on visionary leadership (Knippenberg and Stam: 244), we claim that leader agency is an essential element in both transformational and transactional leadership.

Both leadership strategies can be expected to lead to improved performance (especially in combination), but this paper focuses on transactional leadership (while primarily using transformational leadership as a control variable) for two reasons. First, as discussed in the introduction this is where the controversy is in Public Administration. Several studies have shown positive effects of transformational leadership (e.g. Bellé, 2013; Moynihan et al., 2012), but as we will discuss in more detail below, the evidence is far less clear-cut for transactional leadership. Instead of unfounded rejection of the transactional leadership strategy, this paper contributes with a test of its usefulness in a context where some leaders have started to use it while others have not. And this variation leads us to the second reason for focusing on transactional leadership: It varies. Especially when we use leaders' self-assessments (as we do in this paper to avoid common source bias in our analysis of employee self-efficacy), there is little variation in transformational leadership. Almost all leaders rate themselves as being very transformational, while there is much more variation in their statement concerning transactional leadership. This might even relate back to the first reason to focus on transactional leadership: Even the leaders know that it is more *comme il faut* to use transformational leadership rather than transactional leadership, making social desirability bias much stronger for transformational leadership.

So what do we know about the effects of transactional leadership in public organizations? The strongest argument against using this leadership strategy is found in self-determination theory. The argument is that contingent rewards and punishments reduced satisfaction of the basic needs for autonomy, relatedness and competence – especially the last-mentioned. This means that employee motivation becomes less autonomous and therefore less effective in terms of obtaining high performance (Gagné & Deci, 2005; Deci & Ryan 2000). This is a powerful argument and has (as discussed below) been decisive in terms of including self-efficacy in this paper to analyze whether transformational leadership does indeed mean impaired belief in one's competence for the employees.

If we look at the generic management and leadership literature, the findings are generally more positive (Avolio et al. 2009; Bass et al. 2003; Lowe et al 1996). Contingent reward as the first part of the transactional leadership strategy appears to have a general positive association with performance also in public organizations, but Lowe et al (1996) also find that management-by-exception has a low, but perhaps meaningful, positive relationship with subordinate perceptions of effectiveness in public organizations across studies. It has been argued that transactional leadership is not useful in environments which are changing, but Vigoda-Gadot and Beeri (2013) still find a positive relationship between transactional leadership and change-oriented organizational citizen behavior. Oberfield (2014) also finds that improvements in transformational and transactional leadership, separately and together, are positive predictors of follower cooperation, job satisfaction, and perceptions of work quality. Specifically, Oberfield (2014: 422) find that although transformational leadership appears to be more powerful, improvements in transactional leadership is still estimated to be associated with improvement in perceptions of work quality, cooperation and job satisfaction. Trottier et al. (2008) argues that both contingent reward and management-by-exception are important for perceived leadership effectiveness and employee satisfaction. They find that contingent reward is systematically more important than management-by-exception, and that transformational leadership is more important than the two types of transactional leadership. Finally, Park and Rainey (2008) find weak effects of transaction-oriented leadership on extrinsic motivation, but no effect on employee job satisfaction. In sum, these findings are mixed, and the mixed results on job satisfaction might indicate that employee need satisfaction and therefore self-efficacy might be important.

While several studies have investigated (and found) that employee self-efficacy mediates the relationship between transformational leadership and different performance-related outcomes (e.g. Pillai & Williams 2004; Gong et al. 2009; Nielsen et al. 2009), this has not to our knowledge been analyzed for transactional leadership. Ryan and Deci, who are the founding fathers of self-determination theory, equate the level of perceived competence to self-efficacy for a given activity (2000: 69), and they argue that social-contextual events (e.g. feedback, communications and rewards) that conduce toward feelings of competence during action can enhance intrinsic motivation for that action (2000:70). Their argument is that positive performance feedback enhances intrinsic motivation, whereas negative performance feedback diminishes it. Vallerand and Reid (1984) have further shown that these effects were mediated by perceived competence (which we see as a synonymy to self-efficacy). Given that use of contingent rewards can be seen as positive feedback and that the use of management-by-exception must be seen as negative feedback, the implications of this research is that we should expect self-efficacy to mediate the association between transformational leadership and performance positively for contingent rewards and negatively for management-by-exception. This expectation is formulated as three testable hypotheses below.

> H1: The leaders' use of contingent rewards is positively related to employee self-efficacy
>
> H2: The leader's use of management-by-exception is negatively related to employee self-efficacy
>
> H3: Employee self-efficacy is positively related to organizational performance

Given that transactional leadership is hardly the only determinant of self-efficacy and that self-efficacy is not the only determinant of organizational performance, it is relevant to consider relevant control variables. We have already indicated that we include transformational leadership as the other main part of the Full Range Leadership Theory. As mentioned, a previous study has found a correlation between transformational leadership and self-efficacy (Pillai & Williams 2004), and several studies indicate that transformational leadership affects performance (e.g. Bellé 2013). Given that transformational leadership tends to be positively correlated with the use of contingent rewards, it is very important to control for this variable when we investigate the relationships between transactional leadership strategies, self-efficacy and performance. It is also important to include personal characteristics of both employees and leaders such as age, gender, and experience. These variables may affect the use of the leadership strategies (e.g. Eagly et al. 2003), self-efficacy (e.g. Bausch et al. 2014) and performance (e.g. Kim 2005). Especially in relation to self-efficacy and performance, identification with the relevant profession can also be relevant, because a strong link to an occupation with specialized, theoretical knowledge and firm professional norms can strengthen employees' perceived capabilities to organize and execute the courses of action (that is, their self-efficacy), and it might also lead to better organizational performance to have employees with a high average identification with the relevant profession, because it can increase compliance with professional norms, thus strengthening the professional quality of their work. In the literature, professional identification has before been conceptualized as membership of the professional association (Perry 1997) and we follow this conceptualization. In analyses of self-efficacy, it is also relevant to control for the strength of labor marked connection of the employees (i.e. full time or part time) and for relevant variations in the tasks performed by the employees. At the organizational level, it is relevant to include the number of employees (to account for economies or diseconomies of scale) and for the difficulty of the task (for example for teaching, the most relevant factor here is the socio-demographic composition of the students).

Research design

We test the hypothesis for upper secondary schools in Denmark. The design is cross-sectional, but the multilevel structure of the data with both principals and employees allows us to measure leadership and self-efficacy using separate data sources. Similarly, performance is measured using register data with external evaluation of student academic skills, and the risk of common source bias is therefore low.

The schools are publicly owned and funded, and this area is useful for testing the relevance of leadership and self-efficacy for at least four reasons. First, employees (teachers) and their leader (the school principal) can be linked in a relatively straightforward way, since the principals are responsible for personnel management for all teachers at a given school. Second, Danish upper secondary schools produce more or less identical services, which allows us to keep a number of potentially confounding variables constant and to compare them on their added value to student grades. Third, principals in this area have substantial autonomy given that the schools are self-governing, so they are in a position to exert active leadership. Fourth and finally, simultaneously gathered survey data is available for both leaders (school principals) and employees (teachers), and it is possible to link this survey data to register data on student grades which is an important performance dimension for Danish upper secondary schools.

In the Danish school system, the first ten years of basic schooling (*grundskole*) are mandatory (grades 0 through 9). After basic schooling, the students can continue their education in either a vocational school or a high school. This study focuses on high schools, which provide nationally regulated, tuition-free, general education to more than half of the Danish youth (around 65.000 students in 2010 according to The Ministry of Children and Education, 2010). The schools fall into three categories: 1) The General Upper Secondary Education Program (Stx), 2) The Higher Commercial Examination Program (Hhx), and 3) The Higher Technical Examination Program (Htx) (from hereon 1. General program, 2. Business program, and 3. Technical program). The general program offers a range of subjects in the fields of the natural and social sciences as well as humanities, the business program focuses on business and economic disciplines in combination with general subjects, and the technical program focuses on technological and scientific subjects in combination with general subjects (Ministry of Education, 2014). Thus, the focus varies between schools, but they share the common objective of ensuring students general education, knowledge and competences, and they all qualify for access to higher education. Importantly, the grades given in the shared subjects (such as Danish and Math) are highly comparable.

All three school types have relatively high levels autonomy and are self-governing with their own supervisory boards. They are financed through activity-based budgeting (based on the number of students enrolled and passing exams). Thus, school principals in all three school types are in relatively strong formal positions to exert their leadership. Internally, the schools all have a relatively flat structure with short distance from principal to the teachers. Thus, principals have personnel management responsibility for the teachers, and most of them interact with the teachers on a daily basis. There are middle managers, but their tasks are mainly administrative. On this background there is good reason to expect that principals can exert influence on school performance through the teachers.

Data

We have approached all 135 STX, 38 HTX, and 60 HHX schools in Denmark with an invitation to participate in two parallel surveys directed at the managerial level and the employee level respectively. In October 2012 we sent a letter to the schools, where we requested contact information for principals, middle managers and teachers. Most schools sent us the information, and for most of the remaining schools, we were able to gather information from their websites. More than 60 schools were left out of the investigation either because they actively refused to participate, or because we could not obtain contact information. In late November, we sent web-based questionnaires to 161 principals and 10,471 teachers, and throughout December we sent four reminders to those, who had not yet responded. When the survey was closed on December 21st, 95 principals and 2,271 teachers had replied to the survey (response rates 60.3 percent and 34.1 percent respectively). 91 principal responses were complete (four principals had skipped parts of the questionnaire), and we use these and the 1,921 teachers with complete answers at these schools in the analyses below.

Measures

Most variables under study here were measured with responses from the two questionnaires to employees (teachers) and leaders (school principals only). We have combined employee and leader responses into a multilevel dataset. Before the actual survey, we ran a pilot study to 150 employees and one leader, which resulted in adjustments of the surveys. Primarily, the survey was shortened, but the wording of some items was also changed. In this study, transformational leadership and transactional leadership are measured among leaders, but we have also measured the concept among the teachers. This generally gives stronger associations with self-efficacy, but we do not report them due to the risk of common source bias. We know that leaders' self-ratings tend to be inflated (Fleenor et al., 2010), but there is no reason to expect any bias in the rating (separate from the leadership strategy in itself) to be positively correlated with employee self-efficacy. If anything, differences between employee and leader assessments of the leaders' behavior tend to be detrimental to employee variables similar to self-efficacy (Bass & Yammarino 1991), making our test conservative.

Teacher self-efficacy is conceptualized as the teachers' belief in their capabilities to student academic skills, and this is measured using three internationally validated items from the TALIS surveys (based on question 31 in OECD (2008)) and a self-constructed item (item 4), which has replaces a TALIS item, which did not function in our setting. All items are measures from 1 (totally disagree) to 5 (totally agree) so that high scores are high self-efficacy. As can be seen in table 1, the mean is generally high for all four items, leading to a left-screwed measure, but the factor scores are satisfactory and so is Cronbach's alpha (0.82). When we compute an index for self-efficacy, the mean is 79.44, and the standard deviation is 14.06, indicating that it is not problematically censored.

Table 1: Items measuring Teacher self-efficacy

	M	SD	Factor score
1. I feel that I am making a significant educational difference in the lives of my students	4.22	0.74	0.66
2. I usually know how to get through to students	4.28	0.68	0.79
3. I am successful with the students in my class	4.02	0.67	0.75
4. I am able to get silence in the class when necessary	4.19	0.79	0.66

For transactional leadership, items[1] were taken from Trottier et al. (2008) and Den Hartog et al. (1997). For transformational leadership, items[2] were taken from Podsakoff et al. (1996), Trottier et al. (2008), and Wright et al. (2012) (factor analyses are available on request). Most of the control variables are collected in the surveys (age, gender, and experience of both employees and leader and membership of the professional association, part time employment and whether they teach natural science for the employees, but the number of employees comes from our lists of respondents, which cover all teachers at each school, and information about the socio-demographic composition of the students at the school level comes from register information from Statistics Denmark.

The performance measure applied here is school added value to student grades. We have obtained exam mark information from highly reliable registers. Statistics Denmark thus collects data on all Danish high school students' exam marks. "The observed grade level" is the school means of all externally graded written exams. "The expected grade level" is then calculated based on social demographic variables at the school level (gender, birth year, parents' education level, parents' income (in DKK), parents' employment, parents' age and ethnicity). The school added value to student grades is then calculated as the expected grade level subtracted

---

[1] The items measuring contingent rewards was (1) As a leader, I reward my employees' performance (e.g. through wage supplements), when they live up to expectations and (2) As a leader, reward(s)the employees dependent on how well they perform their jobs. The items measuring contingent punishment was: As a leader, I focus attention on irregularities, mistakes, exceptions and deviations from what is expected of me and (2) As a leader, I dismiss teachers, if they over a longer period do not perform satisfactory.

[2] The items measuring transformational leadership was: (1) As a leader, I provide a compelling vision of the organization's future, (2) As a leader, I articulate and generate enthusiasm for a shared vision and mission, (3) As a leader, I facilitate the acceptance of common goals for the school, (4) As a leader, I say things that make employees proud to be part of the organization.

from the observed grade level, resulting in positive school added value to student grades, if observed grade levels are higher than expected and vice versa. In other words, the performance measure (school added value to student grades) is positive if student exam marks are higher than should be expected based on the students' background and negative if student exam marks are lower than should be expected.

Table 2 shows the summary statistics and correlation between the variables under study.

Table 2. Correlation information (teacher level)

	Variable	Mean	S.D.	Min	Max	(1)	(2)	(3)	(4)	(5)	(6)	(7)
(1)	Self-efficacy	79.44	14.06	0.00	100.00	1.000						
(2)	Contingent reward	68.44	21.00	0.00	100.00	0.040	1.000					
(3)	Management-by-exception	40.39	22.61	0.00	75.00	-0.003	0.149	1.000				
(4)	Transformational leadership	80.36	12.36	31.25	100.00	0.016	0.048	0.106	1.000			
(5)	Teacher age (years)	45.66	11.13	24.00	71.00	-0.020	0.026	-0.007	-0.021	1.000		
(6)	Gender (m = 1)	0.51	0.50	0.00	1.00	0.001	-0.043	-0.043	-0.029	-0.123***	1.000	
(7)	Natural science teacher	0.21	0.41	0.00	1.00	-0.059	0.053	-0.007	0.037	0.034***	-0.143***	1.000
(8)	Part time employment	0.82	0.39	0.00	1.00	0.066	0.001	0.029	-0.009	-0.088***	-0.037	-0.045
(9)	Professional association	0.94	0.23	0.00	1.00	0.099***	-0.016	0.011	0.003	0.072	0.068	0.015
(10)	Socio-demographic index	6.66	0.50	4.70	7.88	0.061	-0.041	0.040	0.084***	-0.060	0.049	0.034
(11)	School size (# teachers)	88.31	36.45	18.00	164.00	-0.026	0.160***	0.192***	0.035	0.079***	-0.013	-0.079***
(12)	Principal age	57.39	6.19	42.00	69.00	0.031	0.045	0.179***	0.162***	-0.040	-0.010	0.013
(13)	Principal gender	0.20	0.40	0.00	1.00	0.003	0.125***	-0.011	0.057	-0.021	-0.070	0.029
(14)	Principal leader experience (years)	17.48	8.69	0.00	38.00	0.015	0.182***	0.056	0.096***	-0.049	0.009	0.045
(15)	General program	0.72	0.45	0.00	1.00	0.006	0.029	-0.096***	0.021	-0.098***	0.009	0.181***
(16)	Business program	0.23	0.42	0.00	1.00	0.012	-0.022	-0.043	-0.154***	0.055	0.050	-0.206***
(17)	Technical program	0.05	0.22	0.00	1.00	-0.035	-0.016	0.273***	0.248***	0.094***	-0.112***	0.024
(18)	School added value to student grades	-0.01	0.08	-0.24	0.23	0.056	0.047	0.024	0.083***	-0.042	-0.023	0.040

Table 1 (continued). Correlation information (teacher level)

	Variable	(8)	(9)	(10)	(11)	(12)	(13)	(14)	(15)	(16)	(17)
(8)	Part time employment	1.000									
(9)	Professional association	0.128***	1.000								
(10)	Socio-demographic index	0.002	0.046	1.000							
(11)	School size (# teachers)	0.023	-0.060	-0.060	1.000						
(12)	Principal age	-0.003	0.029	0.209***	0.125***	1.000					
(13)	Principal gender	-0.012	0.027	-0.078***	-0.022	0.040	1.000				
(14)	Principal leader experience (years)	-0.006	0.029	0.269***	-0.021	0.633***	-0.220***	1.000			
(15)	General program	-0.013	0.144***	0.475***	-0.307***	0.181***	0.139***	0.244***	1.000		
(16)	Business program	-0.004	-0.127***	-0.403***	0.234***	-0.184***	-0.259***	-0.212***	-0.870***	1.000	
(17)	Technical program	0.035	-0.050	-0.198***	0.177***	-0.018	0.208***	-0.092***	-0.376***	-0.130***	1.000
(18)	School added value to student grades	0.025	0.073	0.144***	-0.385***	0.070	0.169***	0.144***	0.113***	-0.178***	0.111***

Methods of analysis

In this study of the relationship between leadership, self-efficacy and organizational performance, we use multi-level regression analysis, since our data is hierarchically structured with information about leadership from the school principals (school level), information about self-efficacy from the teachers (employee level) and information about performance from registers (school level). Unless we use multilevel technics, auto-correlation would lead to potential biases (i.e. teachers within schools teachers have the same leader and their self-efficacy probably tends to be more similar). By controlling for such factors as the socioeconomic composition of students, leader characteristics, and school characteristics, some problems of auto-correlation can be avoided. However, as many factors are unobservable and therefore cannot be controlled for, using standard OLS regression would potentially have resulted in biased standard errors and significance tests (Andersen 2007; Hsiao 2003; Rabe-Hesketh and Skrondal 2008).

As mentioned, we control for a number of variables which might confound the investigated relationships, and some of the personal characteristics included as control variables (age, gender, and experience) are also known to be associated with inflation in self-assessment, reduces the problem of using self-reported leadership strategies of the principals. We have prioritized to use information from the employees on their self-efficacy and information from principals about leadership strategies, since common source bias could otherwise introduce common variance between our measures, which is attributable to unobservable variables and not to actual co-variance (Podsakoff et al., 2003). This has recently been shown to be a serious problem, especially in relation to studies of organizational performance (e.g. Meier & O'Toole 2013).

Results

The results section is divided into two parts. First, we look at how the leaders' reported use of transactional (and transformational) leadership strategies are related to the employees' self-efficacy. Second, we see how leadership strategies and self-efficacy are related to organizational performance (school added value to student grades).

First, the empty model in table 3 confirms that auto-correlation is indeed a potential problem in data, since there is significant variance in self-efficacy between schools. This indicates that the use of a random intercept model is appropriate, i.e. school factors are important for explaining self-efficacy. Given the results from the empty models, all main analyses of self-efficacy include random intercepts to control for school specific effects. These analyses have also been performed with OLS regression with cluster robust standard errors. As using OLS regression unambiguously strengthens the findings, we show only the estimates from the multilevel models. Model 2.1 shows that some control variables are related to self-efficacy. Thus, self-efficacy is reported to be much lower among natural science teachers, much higher among members of the relevant professional association, and also higher in schools with a stronger social demographic composition.

Model 2 and 3 in table 3 show that of the three investigated leadership variables only contingent reward is significantly related to the employees' self-efficacy, and that the relationship is positive. Thus, the results indicate that the more a principal reports to use contingent rewards, the higher self-efficacy do the teachers at the principals' school report. Neither management-by-exception nor transformational leadership is significantly related to self-efficacy. This means that the results support hypothesis 1 (saying that the leaders' use of contingent rewards is positively related to employee self-efficacy) and run counter to hypothesis 2 (saying that the leader's use of management-by-exception is negatively related to employee self-efficacy).

Table 3. Multilevel regressions of teacher self-efficacy. Random intercept.

	Empty model	Model 1	Model 2	Model 3
Contingent reward			0.0413*	0.0407*
			(2.31)	(2.24)
Management-by-exception			-0.00791	-0.00776
			(-0.58)	(-0.57)
Transformational leadership				0.00998
				(0.34)
Teacher level variable				
Age (years)		-0.0227	-0.0244	-0.0241
		(-0.55)	(-0.60)	(-0.59)
Gender (m = 1, f= 0)		-0.494	-0.476	-0.475
		(-0.83)	(-0.80)	(-0.80)
Natural science teacher (dummy)		-1.849*	-1.919*	-1.920*
		(-2.20)	(-2.27)	(-2.27)
Part time employment (dummy)		1.840	1.825	1.831
		(1.94)	(1.93)	(1.94)
Professional association (dummy)		5.947***	5.985***	5.985***
		(3.46)	(3.49)	(3.50)
School level variables				
Socio-demographic index		2.133*	2.316*	2.285*
		(2.17)	(2.48)	(2.47)
School size (# teachers)		-0.0100	-0.0152	-0.0154
		(-0.85)	(-1.38)	(-1.44)
Principal age (years)		0.0925	0.128	0.125
		(1.18)	(1.62)	(1.53)
Principal gender (m =1, f = 0)		0.505	-0.0603	-0.0526
		(0.50)	(-0.06)	(-0.05)
Principal's leader experience (years)		-0.0330	-0.0716	-0.0707
		(-0.67)	(-1.49)	(-1.46)
General program		1.038	0.403	0.566
		(0.55)	(0.21)	(0.29)
Business program		3.304	2.709	2.865
		(1.63)	(1.38)	(1.41)
Technical program		(ref)	(ref)	(ref)
Constant	79.51***	54.41***	50.56***	50.01***
	(212.74)	(6.91)	(6.63)	(6.31)
N groups	91	91	91	91
N observations	1.921	1,921	1,921	1,921
R^2 within	0.0000	0.01961	0.0192	0.0192
R^2 between	0.0000	0.0754	0.1269	0.1216
R^2 overall	0.0000	0.0238	0.0273	0.0275
Sigma_u	2.0196	2.0754	1.8283	1.8652
Sigma_e	13.9698	13.8587	13.8625	13.8625
Rho	0.02047	0.02194	0.01710	0.01778

Note: * $p < 0.05$, ** $p < 0.01$, *** $p < 0.001$. Unstandardized regression coefficients (t statistics in parentheses)

Next, we turn to the relationships between leadership, self-efficacy and organizational performance. These results are made on aggregated school data, since the dependent variable, school added value to student grades, is only available at school level. Thus, the dataset has been collapsed at school level, and mean scores for the teacher level variables have been calculated. Model 1 in table 4 shows that none of the leadership strategies are significantly related to school added value to student grades. There is, however, a positive relationship with the share of unionized teachers, a negative relationship with school size, and school added value to student grades is lower at the general program (maybe because students with higher socio-economic status tend to choose this program in the first place, making it more difficult for this type of program to exceed expected grades given the students' background). These results should generally not be interpreted as causal relationships, since selection issues may play a serious role. The coefficients only change little between model 2 and model 3 in table 4, where self-efficacy is introduced. The results show that despite the small sample, self-efficacy is significantly and positively related to organizational performance (school added value to student grades). Thus, the higher the mean self-efficacy score of teachers in a given school is, the higher school value added is. Although we cannot be sure that this is causal relationship, the dependent variable is measures the year after we measured teacher self-efficacy to make sure that the high level of self-efficacy is not a result of high student grades in the previous exam. It is possible that the schools which in general perform well also attract and select more teachers with high self-efficacy, but the results can at least be seen as an indication that the expected effect of self-efficacy on organizational performance exists for Danish upper secondary schools (thus supporting hypothesis 3).

Table 4. OLS regressions of school added value to student grades (2013) by leadership and self-efficacy (2012)

	Model 1	Model 2	Model 3
Self-efficacy			0.00493*
			(2.00)
Contingent reward		0.000401	0.000148
		(0.92)	(0.33)
Management-by-exception		-0.0000391	-0.00000169
		(-0.08)	(-0.00)
Transformational leadership		-0.000545	-0.000688
		(-0.79)	(-1.04)
Mean teacher age (years)	-0.000719	-0.000925	-0.000583
	(-0.27)	(-0.30)	(-0.19)
% male	-0.0220	-0.0262	-0.00890
	(-0.35)	(-0.40)	(-0.13)
% in professional association	0.269*	0.293*	0.275*
	(2.13)	(2.16)	(2.04)
School size (# teachers)	-0.000668*	-0.000648*	-0.000593
	(-2.27)	(-2.09)	(-1.86)
Principal age (years)	-0.0000930	-0.0000220	-0.000428
	(-0.05)	(-0.01)	(-0.21)
Principal gender (m =1, f = 0)	0.0134	0.00776	0.0179
	(0.61)	(0.32)	(0.78)
Principal's leader experience (years)	0.000874	0.000747	0.00107
	(0.67)	(0.49)	(0.70)
General program	-0.0629*	-0.0755*	-0.0854*
	(-2.24)	(-2.19)	(-2.16)
Business program	-0.0288	-0.0401	-0.0507
	(-0.95)	(-1.07)	(-1.15)
Technical program	(ref)	(ref)	(ref)
Constant	-0.120	-0.102	-0.453
	(-0.63)	(-0.42)	(-1.49)
N	87	87	87
R^2	0.131	0.145	0.182
adj. R^2	0.029	0.007	0.037

Note: * $p < 0.05$, ** $p < 0.01$, *** $p < 0.001$. (t statistics in parentheses)

Discussion and conclusion

The research question was how transactional leadership strategies relate to employee self-efficacy in public organizations, and how self-efficacy relates to organizational performance. In our multilevel study of Danish upper secondary schools, we find that the use of contingent rewards is positively associated with higher self-efficacy among the teachers, while we cannot identify an association for management-by-exception. Concerning the second part of the question, we find that the average self-efficacy of the teachers is positively related to organizational performance controlled for relevant variables concerning the student, the teachers and the principals. These findings give rise to two main questions: How far can they be generalized, and are we talking about causal effects in the sense that the use of rewards increases self-efficacy which again increases organizational performance.

Danish high school teachers form a relatively professionalized group with a general negative attitude towards the use of pecuniary rewards. Both characteristics should be expected to decrease a potential positive effect of contingent rewards, because professional norms are another potential determinant of behavior (and therefore performance), and because motivation crowding theory (Frey 1997) suggests that a controlling perception of an incentive system should make the effect less positive on performance (or even make the net effect negative). In this way, our case can be seen as conservative. On the other hand, the autonomy of the school principals is relatively high, indicating that rewards can at least be used without interference from other hierarchical levels. It would be highly useful to analyze the usefulness of rewards as a transactional leadership strategy in other countries and in other sectors, but this study contributes with the message that this type of leadership should not be automatically excluded from consideration. Transactional strategies might be harmful in *some* public organizations (Moynihan, 2010; Perry et al., 2009), but our results indicate that it is not always the case. We introduced self-efficacy as a potential mediator, because we argued that rewards might serve as a mechanism for highlighting the goals and contributions to these goals for the individual employees and thus increasing their feeling of competence. Our results indicate that this is a plausible mechanism for the relationship between transactional leadership and organizational performance, but it should also be noted that there is no direct, significant relationship between use of contingent rewards and organizational performance (although both are positively associated with self-efficiency). There can be several interpretations. One is that the mediated effect is too weak to identify with a sample of relatively few organizations. Another is that contingent rewards can have a direct negative effect on performance, but that this is neutralized by an indirect effect of self-efficacy. Our results with positive (but insignificant) associations between the use of rewards and performance in analyses both including and excluding self-efficacy suggest that this is not the case. Finally, a last interpretation could be that the use of rewards is not important at all for organizational performance. The relatively modest size of the significant associations combined with the lack of direct association between use of rewards and organizational performance suggest that it is not a vital factor.

So what are the implications – if any – for managers and for future research? The results cannot be used to recommend either using or not using contingent rewards, but if part of the literature has one-sidedly spoken against the use of contingent rewards in the public sector, our results can be used to show that this is not always the whole story. In terms of future research, we argue that our findings suggest that it is fruitful to continue research on different types of leadership strategies, including contingent rewards, and to use research designs which (like in this paper) decrease the risk of common source bias while also optimizing the possibilities to make causal inference. That can for example be done in experimental research. Until then, we argue that the main contribution of this paper is to show that self-efficacy can be an important mechanism, given that it can be linked to both conditional rewards and performance. Although we cannot give a final answer on how to obtain employees with high self-efficacy, our results suggest that the use of contingent rewards can be a way to do it, and they also indicate that it can actually be important to focus on self-efficacy because we find a significant and positive association between this concept and organizational performance.

References

Andersen, L. B., & Pallesen, T. (2008). "'Not Just for the Money?' How financial incentives affect the number of publications at Danish Research Institutions". *International Public Management Journal*, 11: 28–47.

Andersen, S.C. 2007. "Multilevel-Modeller: En Introduktion Og et Eksempel. *Politica*no. 3: 294–316.

Antonakis, J. & R. House (2013). A re-analysis of the full-range leadership theory: The way forward, Transformational and Charismatic Leadership: the Road Ahead, 10th Anniversary Ed., Monographs in Leadership and Management, 5: 35.37.

Avolio, B.J., R.J. Reichard, S.T. Hannah, F.O. Walumbwa, A. Chan (2009). A meta-analytic review of leadership impact research: Experimental and quasi-experimental studies, Leadership Quarterly, 20: 764-784.

Bandura, A. (1997). *Self-Efficacy: The Exercise of Control*. New York: W. H. Freeman.

Bass, B.; Avolio, B. J.; Jung, D. I.; Berson, Y. (2003). Predicting Unit Performance by Assessing Transformational and Transactional Leadership, *Journal of Applied Psychology*, 88 (2): 207-18.

Bass, Bernard M., & Riggio, R. E. (2006). *Transformational leadership* (2nd ed.). Mahwah, NJ: Lawrence Erlbaum.

Bass, B. M. and Yammarino, F. J. (1991), Congruence of Self and Others' Leadership Ratings of Naval Officers for Understanding Successful Performance. *Applied Psychology: An International Review*, 40: 437–454

Bausch, S., Michel, A. and Sonntag, K. (2014), How gender influences the effect of age on self-efficacy and training success. Online before print *International Journal of Training and Development*. doi: 10.1111/ijtd.12027

Bellé, N. (2013). Leading to Make a Difference: A Field Experiment on the Performance Effects of Transformational Leadership, Perceived Social Impact, and Public Service Motivation. *Journal of Public Administration Research and Theory*. Online before print. doi: 10.1093/jopart/mut033

Deci, E.L. & R.M. Ryan (2000). The "What" and "Why" of Goal Pursuits: Human Needs and Self-determination of Behavior, *Psychological Inquiry*, 11 (4): 227-68.

Eagly AH, Johannesen-Schmidt MC, van Engen ML (2003) Transformational, transactional, and laissez-faire leadership styles: A meta-analysis comparing women and men. *Psychological Bulletin* 129(4):569-591

Frey, B. 1997. *Not just for the money. An Economic Theory of Personal Motivation*. Cheltenham and Brookfield: Edward Elgar Publishing.

Gagné, M. and E. L. Deci. 2005. "Self-determination theory and work motivation." *Journal of Organizational Behavior* 26: 331-362.

Gong, Yaping; Jia-Chi Huang, and Jiing-Lih Farh (2009) Employee Learning Orientation, Transformational Leadership, and Employee Creativity: The Mediating Role of Employee Creative Self-Efficacy *Academy of Management Journal* 52:4 765-778.

Hartog, D. N., Muijen, J. J. and Koopman, P.L. (1997) Transactional versus transformational leadership: An analysis of the MLQ. *Journal of occupational and organizational psychology*, 70: 1 pp19–34.

Heinrich, C. J. & G. Marschke. 2010 "Incentives and Their Dynamics in Public Sector Performance Management Systems". *Journal of Policy Analysis and Management* 29(1): 183-208.

Hooijberg, R., & Choi, J. (2001). The impact of organizational characteristics on leadership effectiveness models: An examination of leadership in a private and a public sector organization. *Administration & Society*, 33: 403-431.

Hsiao, C. 2003. *Analysis of Panel Data*. Cambridge: Cambridge University Press.

Holmstrom, B. (1979). Moral hazard and observability, *Bell Journal of Economics*, 10(1): 74-91.

Jacobsen, C.B. & L.B. Andersen (forthcoming). Performance Management in the Public Sector. Does it Decrease or Increase Innovation and Performance? *International Journal of Public Administration*.

Judge, T. A., & Piccolo, R. F. (2004). Transformational and transactional leadership: A meta-analytic test of their relative validity. *Journal of Applied Psychology*, 89: 755-768.

Kellough, J. E. and H. Lu. 1993. The Paradox of Merit Pay in the Public Sector: Persistence of a Problematic Procedure. *Review of Public Personnel Administration* 13(2): 45-64.

Kim, S.(2005) Individual-Level Factors and Organizational Performance in Government Organizations *Journal of Public Administration Research & Theory* 15:245–261

Langbein, L. (2010). Economics, Public Service Motivation, and Pay for Performance: Complements or Substitutes?, *International Public Management Journal*, 13: 1, 9 — 23

Lawler, E.E. (1990). *Strategic pay: Aligning organizational strategies and pay systems*, San Francisco: Jossey Bass.

Le Grand, J. (2003): *Motivation, Agency and Public Policy: Of Knights and Knaves, Pawns and Queens*. Oxford: Oxford University Press.

Lowe, K. B., Kroeck, K. G., & Sivasubramaniam, M. (1996). Effectiveness correlates of transformational and transactional leadership: A meta-analytic review of the MLQ literature. *The Leadership Quarterly*, 7: 385-425.

Meier, Kenneth J., and Laurence J. O'Toole. 2013. Subjective organizational performance and measurement error: Common source bias and spurious relationships. *Journal of Public Administration Research and Theory* 23 (2): 429-456.

Moe, T.M. 1984. The New Economics of Organization. *American Journal of Political Science,* 28 (4): 739–777.

Moynihan, D. P. (2010). A workforce of cynics? The effects of contemporary reforms on public service motivation. *International Public Management Journal*, *13*(1), 24–34.

Moynihan, D. P., Pandey, S. K., & Wright, B. E. (2012). Setting the table: How transformational leadership fosters performance information use. *Journal of Public Administration Research and Theory*, *22*(1), 143–164.

Nielsen, K., Yarker, J., Randall, R., Munir, F. (2009), "The mediating effects of team and self-efficacy on the relationship between transformational leadership, and job satisfaction and psychological well-being in healthcare professionals: a cross-sectional questionnaire survey", *International Journal of Nursing Studies*, 46 (9): 1236-1244.

Oberfield, Z. W. (2014). Public Management in Time: A Longitudinal Examination of the Full Range of Leadership Theory. *Journal of Public Administration Research and Theory*. 24 (2): 407-429

OECD (2008) *OECD Teaching and Learning International Survey (TALIS) Teacher questionnaire* http://www.oecd.org/edu/school/TALIS%202008%20Questionnaires.pdf accessed July 9th 2014

Park, S.M. & H.G. Rainey (2008). Leadership and Public Service Motivation in U.S. Federal Agencies, *International Journal of Public Managament*, 11 (1): 109-42.

Perry, James L. (1997) Antecedents of Public Service Motivation *Journal of Public Administration Research and Theory*, 7 (2): 181-197.

Perry, James L. & Lois R. Wise (1990). The motivational bases of Public Service, *Public Administration Review, 50*(3): 367-73.

Perry, J. L., T. Engbers and S. Yun Jun. 2009. "Back to the Future? Performance-Related Pay, Empirical Research, and the Perils of Persistence." *Public Administration Review* 68 (1): 39-51.

Pillai, R., & Williams, E.A. (2004) Transformational leadership, self-efficacy, group cohesiveness, commitment, and performance. *Journal of Organizational Change Management*, 17, 144–159.

Podsakoff, P.M., MacKenzie, S.B. and Bommer, W.H. (1996) Meta-analysis of the relationships between Kerr and Jermier's substitutes for leadership and employee job attitudes, role perceptions, and performance. *Journal of Applied Psychology*, 81: 4 pp380-99.

Podsakoff, P.M.; MacKenzie, S.B.; Lee, J.-Y.; Podsakoff, N.P. (2003). Common method biases in behavioral research: A critical review of the literature and recommended remedies. *Journal of Applied Psychology* 88 (5): 879–903.

Rabe-Hesketh, S., and A. Skrondal. 2008. *Multilevel and Longitudinal Modeling Using Stata*. College Station, TX: STATA press.

Rainey, H. G. 1982. "Reward Preferences Among Public and Private Managers: In Search of the Service Ethic." *American Review of Public Administration* 16(4): 288–302.

Ryan, Richard M., and Edward L. Deci. "Self-determination theory and the facilitation of intrinsic motivation, social development, and well-being." *American psychologist* 55.1 (2000): 68-78.

Trottier, T., M. Van Wart, and X. Wang. 2008. Examining the nature and significance of leadership in government organizations. *Public Administration Review* 68:319–33.

Vatlerand, R. J., & Reid, G. (1984). On the causal effects of perceived competence on intrinsic motivation: A test of cognitive evaluation theory. *Journal of Sport Psychology*, 6, 94-102.

Van Knippenberg, D., & Sitkin, S. B. (2013). A Critical Assessment of Charismatic—Transformational Leadership Research: Back to the Drawing Board? *The Academy of Management Annals*, 7(1), 1–60.

Van Knippenberg, D. & D. Stam (2014). "Visionary leadership" page 241-259 chapter 12 in D. Day (ed.) *The Oxford Handbook of Leadership and Organizations*. Oxford: Oxford University Press.

Van Wart, M. (2013) Administrative leadership theory: a reassessment after 10 years. *Public Administration*. Online before print. doi: 10.1111/padm.12017

Vigoda-Gadot, E. & I. Beeri (2013), Change-Oriented Organizational Citizenship Behavior in Public Administration: The Power of Leadership and the Cost of Organizational Politics, *Journal of Public Administration Research and Theory*, 22: 573-96.

Wright, B.E. & A.M. Grant (2010). Unanswered Questions about Public Service Motivation: Designing Research to Address Key Issues of Emergence and Effects, *Public Administration Review*, 70 (5): 691-700.

Wright, B. E., Moynihan, D. P. and Pandey, S. K. (2012) Pulling the Levers: Transformational Leadership, Public Service Motivation, and Mission Valence. *Public Administration Review* 72:2 pp206–15.

Yukl, G. (1999). An evaluation of conceptual weaknesses in transformational and charismatic leadership theories, The Leadership Quarterly, 10 (2): 285-305.